PANPSYCHISM

COSMOS AND YOU

सर्बम् प्राणमयं जगत्

by

Rabindranath Haldar

Published by R. N. Haldar through self publishing platform of Notion Press

Printed by Notion Press

Dedication

I dedicate this book to my only daughter Mrs. Aditi Chatterjee, my son-in-law Mr. Aniruddha Chatterjee and my only grandson Aditya Chatterjee - who have since traveled to most places on this planet and everywhere they felt the urge to see the celestial firmament in the clear night sky.

At the top of the list of dedications is my wife Indrani Devi who has always been my shadow companion on this planet and with her our departed son Indrajit.

Acknowledgements - My friend and schoolmate Parames Ghosh - without whom this book would not have been published and I am grateful to my college friend Mr. Lokendra Nath Roychoudury for his help to render computer support.

The author is indebted to Mr. Tanmoy Bera for composing the latest front and back cover of this book.

TABLE OF CONTENTS

Dedication……….….................................. …….......1

Table of Contents……….…..................... …….... ...2

Preface……….…..….….3

Introduction……….…..5

Existence Itself, Consciousness
and Bliss......….……….….....................….…....8

Standard Model of Elementary
Particles......………............. …….…….……….,..14

Vault of Heaven……….…....................................25

Galaxies.......................….…....……......…….......... 29

Nature of Universe:
Quasars. Black holes , Curvature of
Space…….…………………………………….…… .32

Birth And Death of Stars......…………......…… .50

Birth of Universe & Determination
Of time……….…………………….. …….……56

Epilogue…………………….…....................……… ..78

Glossary……………....…………………....…… ..107

PREFACE

Panpsychism proposes that consciousness is a fundamental feature of the universe, present in different forms and at different levels. Panpsychism suggests that consciousness exists at different levels and in different forms. For example, some panpsychists believe that monads, or psychic atoms of energy, have different levels of consciousness. In inorganic matter, monads are sleeping, in animals they are dreaming, and in humans they are awake. Panpsychism is one of the oldest philosophical theories, and has been linked to philosophers like Plato, Thales, and Spinoza. Interest in panpsychism has increased in the 21st century due to developments in psychology, neuroscience, quantum mechanics, and renewed interest in the hard problem of consciousness. So much information is there but it was not mentioned that in ancient Indian scriptures it was believed by way of revelation during *Sadhana* (intense disciplinary and esoteric pursuit of self realisation) that the whole universe is vibrant with *Prana* (vital force) and

Chaitanya (consciousness).   It is evident that without *Prana* (vital force) there cannot be any trace of *Chaitanya* (Consciousness). This was much, much before Plato and other Greek Philosophers.

||सर्बम् प्राणमयं जगत्॥

INTRODUCTION

"What caterpillar calls the end of the world, Master calls it a butterfly. - Richard Bach, Illusions - Adventures of a Reluctant Messiah.

If we change our view a little it becomes natural that we are no more than a formless entity. Seeing is not seeing through eyes only, but seeing is a feeling. Senses in outer covering present, which is only a somewhat especially suitable instrument. We do not hear with our eyes and do not smell with our ears. Each instrument is made for a different action. We have five external senses by which we collect knowledge or experience of various things. Not just collections, these collections are sent to certain higher analysers inside.

The name of that highly powerful sense group Is called *Jnanendriya* or sense organs. But for whom is it sent? Who works with them and if we further enquire using our insight what we find at the end -

some people name the object as *Jivatma*, some say God etc.

The point is that what does the inner being look like for which all sorts of experiences are gathered? Whether outwardly and inwardly the impressions of the senses are fully present in it. It is an imposed and long-standing concept or as a result of a reformatory complex our nature is basically ours and are established in us as senses or instruments. We are subtle beings in this form or are called the *Lingasharir* or subtle body. What is present in the gross body, it is present in the subtle body too but without any gross form. If we exclude the form, we can find that this is nothing but a being only. This is the same for all. All these entities are busy acquiring knowledge of things. It needs eyes, ears, nose, tongue, and skin. Their functions are in gross form. By their innate power they send the experience of the external world to somewhere inside, but to whom they send ? They send them to much finer instruments than what they are and by them the form, taste, sound, smell and touch are felt. The locations of these senses are in our brain. These senses again pick up these messages to send to a more subtle being- whose name is **subtle** body. By means of long-standing impressions or complexes these messages or information are accessed and subsequently analyzed by a much higher and subtle being. The causal form of gross is subtle and the causal form of subtle is this **Being**. Such as trees and its seeds - the tree is coarse and the seed is fine. All the plants themselves exist subtly in their seeds, waiting for manifestation only.

Likewise, it is also reasonable to say that there lies the cause of the seed also. Everything has a cause. When it manifests, its form is revealed. With uncovering of *Avidya* (illusive truth), true knowledge or truth related to objects will be revealed. Who requires this experience, whom to deliver this experience, taking so much trouble? From gross to subtle. Reason of cause is *Mahakaran* (cause of causal) etc. etc.

Our inner soul needs these, because it is also its duty to convey these impressions to ***Kutastha Chaitanya*** (eternal consciousness), or the threshold of consciousness - from where all destinies are controlled by the Supreme Consciousness.There are only two groups of lifeforms that survive independent of all others. One lives by photosynthesis (derives energy from light). The other lives by chemosynthesis (derives energy from superheated hydrothermal vents). All other living creatures live by consuming them, directly or indirectly. The same is applicable to humans as well. But the food of the soul is - **knowledge and bliss**. Which is very subtle. Whatever we do, it is only for knowledge and joy. *Jivatma's* (soul in individual) form is only Existence, mere existence. As long as this feeling exists, I refer to it as *Jivatma*. The cause of life is the supreme soul. Just a sense of existence.

Existence Itself, Consciousness and Bliss

This is about the five senses. Apart from these, the subtle senses (yes, I am mentioning them as senses) present, such as *Chitta* (Conscious vital element*)*, *Manas* (Mind or restless Prana), *Buddhi* (Mental analyser), *Ahamkara* (Idea of separate identity) etc. I call them senses for ease of understanding. They are various forms of attributable consciousness of life force or *PRANA*.

Discussion on consciousness is always subjective and not objective. State of consciousness is extremely subtle on one end and on the other end it becomes as gross as all kinds of matter. In short, everything that we see around us is the transformation of the state of consciousness only. The following stages of consciousness were known by our ancient seers:

i) *Vaiswanar* or *Jagrat* (Wakefulness)

ii) *Taijas* (Dream State)

iii) *Prājna* or *Susupti* (Inconscience or deep sleep)

iv) *Turiya* (Super consciousness)

What do I see ? My body, this house, this writing paper, Sun, Moon, planets and billions of constellations - all these are called inert or Matter.

If we gradually keep disintegrating matter, we will go to its very tiny state having the same properties of the gross matter. It is called a molecule. The molecular properties of iron are similar to those of iron and the properties of molecules of salt are those like salt. This molecule is invisible to the eye. But matter is made of billions of molecules which can be touched and felt. The gross form can also be seen by the eyes also.

Now let's break this molecule further down. In the molecular state compounds retain their own properties.

By breaking molecules, we get atoms such as Hydrogen, Helium, Carbon atoms etc. They have their own characteristics. Because they are Elements.

Two or more elements together make molecular compounds, property or quality of which is present in their own molecules.

It seems to be the removal of the first step among various steps of *avidya* in revealing the real nature of unity from diversity. So far 118 elements have been discovered. Two more are being sought for. Evidence has not yet been from found. All these elements are different from original substances from which they are obtained

Different compounds are created in different elemental combinations. Periodic Table:

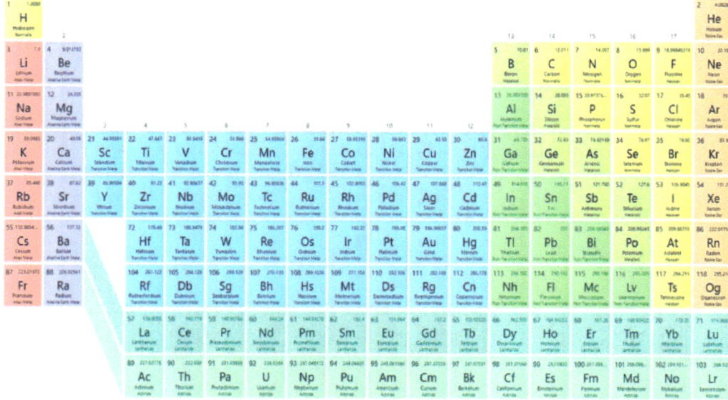

From molecule to atom - in this one step so many compounds are brought down to only 118 constituent elements. As if it is like removing the various apparent looks of so many substances. We shall call them the first step of removal of *Avidya* or illusive truth from actual or real substance. Now as apparent truth, different atoms came to us. On further investigation an atom appeared not indivisible. Atoms consist of finer subatomic particles. In the heart of an atom, a nucleus was discovered and negatively charged electrons revolve around the nucleus. Its mass is extremely less and it is negatively charged electrical objects. Inside the nucleus there resides a positively charged particle named Proton along with an electrically neutral subatomic particle named Neutron.

With different combinations of electrons, protons, neutrons various matters are produced. We can say that this discovery removes the second step of ignorance or *Avidya* in the process of finding Unity from Diversity.

A Hydrogen atom consists of one electron and one Proton. In this way Helium is formed in different combinations, and thus Ozone, Oxygen, Phosphorus, Ferric or iron, Silica or sand, etc. also formed.

Apart from the existence of electrons, protons and neutrons the other subatomic particles like positron, mason, pi mason etc. were discovered. Now on further investigation, the existence of more subtle and mysterious quarks was found. In different combinations of its negative and positive states, they yield electrons, protons, neutrons. The complexities of which are yet to be understood entirely by the scientists. At this stage we have reached the third step in unfolding Ignorance. Now a lot of substances have lost their masked appearance. Scientists are busy studying the mysterious particles called Meon Neutrino formed when cosmic rays strike the atmosphere. These mysterious particles have no mass, have only energy. It is much like an electron without electrical conductivity. These neutrinos pervade the whole universe. There is nothing that can be obstacles in their path.

Prof. Satyendra Nath Bose FRS,

(January 1894 – 4 February 1974) was an Indian theoretical physicist and mathematician. He is best known for his work on quantum mechanics in the early 1920s, in developing the foundation for Bose–Einstein statistics and the theory of the Bose–Einstein condensate. A Fellow of the Royal Society, he was awarded India's second highest civilian award, the Padma Vibhushan, in 1954 by the Government of India.

Standard Model of elementary particles.

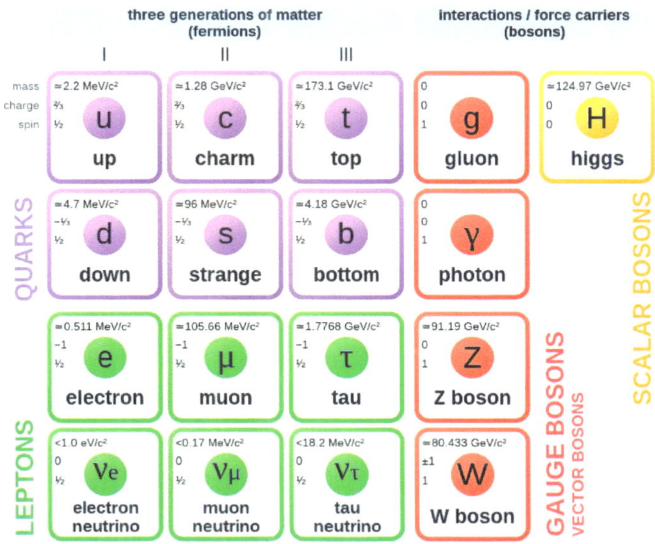

A Boson is an elementary particle with integer spin. This particle obeys Bose-Einstein statistics. The particle was named by Paul Dirac after Satyen Bose (the Bose of Bose-Einstein statistics), the eminent Indian Bengali theoretical physicist and professor of developmental physics at Calcutta University and Dhaka University. Bosons are mostly compound particles.

Examples of bosons are photons, gluons, and the W and Z bosons (the standard model's four force-carrying gauge bosons), the recently discovered Higgs boson, and the hypothesis of quantum gravity. Some composite particles are bosons, such as mesons, and even nuclei of fixed mass number such as deuterium (one proton and one neutron, atomic mass number = 2), for helium 4, and for lead 208; as well as some quasi-particles (e.g. copper pairs, plasmons and phonons).

The last column of the standard list of elementary particles gives the range of boson particles.

Cryogenics is the branch of physics that deals with the production and effects of very low temperatures. The Large Hadron Collider (LHC) is the largest cryogenic system in the world and one of the coldest places on Earth. All of the magnets on the LHC are electromagnets – magnets in which the magnetic field is produced by the flow of electric current. The LHC's main magnets operate at a temperature of 1.9 K (-271.3°C), colder than the 2.7 K (-270.5°C) of outer space.

The LHC's cryogenic system requires 40,000 leak-tight pipe seals, 40 MW of electricity – 10 times more than is needed to power a locomotive – and 120 tonnes of Helium to keep the magnets at 1.9 K.

Scientists have recently divided the substance into two parts.

1. Force particle or force substance.

2. Matter particle is just inert.

It has been proven that Matter and Energy are not different - Just a change of state.

The most amazing thing in this Universe is Light, which is made of Photon particles, which when in motion, has momentum and energy but its rest mass is zero.

The scientists believe in Unified Field Theory which believes all energy originates from One and Single energy and then all matter is born from that energy. To reach unity let us give its name as **CONSCIOUSNESS**.

Leaving the context of the outside world of human beings let us look into their inner world.

The matter eaten every day turns into the body's blood, marrow, bones. It is transformed through cells, the process is called **Metabolism**. As a result, our growth, our energy is generated. Finally, more subtle matter is formed which is unique and indispensable to our brain system and is called — **Cerebrospinal fluid.** First of all, I have said about *Samskara* (past experience or impressions) in connection with the body. Now we will see the role play of this *Samaskra* in our brain system. We are like what we are only due to transformation for millions of years. Before that we existed dormant in the population of apes. Before that we existed in extremely subtle form among marine reptiles.

This evolution was first in reptiles, and then in mammals. The impression of this long journey can be found in our brain system.

Our brain system is built around **R-Complex** or Reptilian Complex or Reptile *Samaskara*. As a result of this Reptilian nature, anger, greed, jealousy, greed, hunger, lust for life etc. are born inside us. The name of the upper layer of the R-Complex is called **Limbic System** or Mammalian Complex or mammalian *Samskara*. The main attributes of which are motherhood, pity, fear, to live socially or collectively etc. Should we assume that only reptilian and mammalian complexes exist in the human brain? Then where is man's own brain?

Surely there is and He is above all.

Which is called the **Seat of Humanity**. Its name is Neocortex, where matter is transformed into consciousness, and for which we are rational.

On one hand, there exists the blind urge of physical and vital being, which seems to be somewhat obscure like inanimate form or matter. It covers a large and extended realm. This is the Reptile Complex. It gets enlightened by the *Chitta* (conscious vital element) , and there comes the Limbic System. Later in the Neocortex, *Manas* or Mind awakens with light and wisdom.

This scientific concept is very modern. I am discussing what has been discovered so far. Intricate analysis of Neocortex is yet a dream to scientists. But to the sages and wise men of India it was revealed long ago. But in this context, it is now irrelevant as this wisdom is conveyed from Master to disciple directly. At present scientists are the sages of today.

It requires a lot of effort to understand their language. Same with the sages and wise men of India ; *Sadhana or* intense practice for pursuit of spiritual understanding is required to grasp the meaning of their revelation. Disagreement does not matter because the truth shall always be truth. It cannot be denied.

However, traces of evolution will remain what we call *Samskara.* This is in our brain and body. Reaching the origin of cells, we find RNA & DNA (ribonucleic and deoxyribonucleic acid) by whose magical power we are like as we are. At the root we find Nucleotides and Amino Acids. The elements present in it are Hydrogen, Oxygen, Carbon and Nitrogen. Hence, we again return to square A. Let us call the final and last stage of cell division Chaitanya or **Cognitive Consciousness.**

We see on the one hand, the subtlest state of matter or inanimate matter is *Para Chaitanya* (Supra Intelligent Conscious Force). There is a difference between consciousness and becoming conscious. On the other hand - *Kutastha* (involved eternal self-effulgence)   *Para   Chaitanya*   (super consciousness) at different levels of material objects. *Chaitanya,* in inanimate matter, is covered by darkness or inconscience.

The last stage of division (or disintegration) of anything is nothing but Consciousness, revealing this universal disclosure. It can be said that the whole universe is Conscious. (सर्बम् प्राणमयं जगत्) This Supreme Consciousness is in all things, but remains as a root in a causal form.

Manifestations of the Universe look different under the mask of illusive truth or *Avidya.* Not only in the presence of **Maya** or Avidya this Consciousness is the matrix of everything. *Chaitanya* is the reservoir. It is consciously indifferent. Existence alone is its nature, expresses itself in relation with the second entity. This is total relativism. We call it **Sadbrahman**. He is everything in the mask of diversity. It is *Ananda* or bliss itself and known as **Sāt** (existence itself), *Chit* (consciousness itself), **Ananda** (bliss itself).

All powerful pure Will for which the universe came into existence, is called ***Iksha*** or ***Kali***.

To do her job well, the individual soul manifests into existence with the covering of *Avidya* on Supreme Consciousness. This **Jivatma** or individual soul is a collector of experience at various level of consciousness.

Subtlety becomes essential for its workings. Idea of separate existence or **Ahamkara** or "I"-ness becomes a prima facie requirement for its existence. It is very subtle and expressive. It needs Intellect - which is indispensable in judging and bringing home a collection of different emotions. Its location is in the brain where the formerly known Neocortex is situated.

For gross reception we need gross instruments, which are called our outer sense organs, as described earlier. We identify *Manas* or mind as a sense organ for its functions for collection of subtler reactive feelings. This is also covered with ignorance.

Then comes a faculty we call *Chitta*, or conscious vital elements. It receives messages from life force or *Prana.* Then comes the body - pure, dark, mostly inconscient and entangled consciousness associated with our bodies.

When this body dies the void part of the five great elements enters into the realm of *Iksha* thereafter returns to *Parachaitanya (*Supreme Consciousness*)*. But due to imperfect *Samskara* (impressions of the past), this does not become complete.

Then we need *Kripa*, which means in other words - grace and mercy. Whose grace? Here comes the door keeper. That pure form of Supramental conscious force of cognitive consciousness or *Chaitanya*, divine Mother of Cosmos manifestation, in Sanskrit we call her *Kali*, the *Iksha* in disguise of *Jaganmata* (divine mother of Cosmos). She looks as if she is helpless. Those who are supposed to obey her orders are acting like bureaucrats, dominating and pampering the wrong and false desires, thus the total system becomes uncoordinated and hence fails to reach unity.

These bureaucrats are mainly *Ahamkar* (idea of separate identity), *Buddhi* (intellect), *Manas* (mind or restless Prana or life force), *Chitta* (conscious vital element) etc. Their duty is to obey the orders of pure *Iksha*. On the contrary they are behaving like anarchists.

The *chitta* is interfering in the course and urge of life. The mind with all its weaknesses, stands before the pure judgment of intellect. We are unable to find the existence and manifestation of *Iksha*. To understand that there is a way but before that I will try to understand the identity of consciousness at every level.

Primary level is dark, inert consciousness — our body. It is built with the help of *Kshiti* (earth), *Ap* (water), *Tej* (fire), *Marut* (wind) and *Byom* (space), the five great elements. The attributes of this layer are - mass and weight, fluidity, energy, airiness and expansion.

Then the development of consciousness occurs in vital, which has feelings of hunger, sleep, thirst, fear of death and sickness.

After that, consciousness develops in higher vital. In other words, it is nothing but a restless mind. It is responsible for anger, greed, infatuation, pride and gluttony etc., etc.

After that comes *Manas* or mind. Its nature manifests itself in love, poetry, valor, greatness and sacrifice. At a more elevated state it manifests kindness, forgiveness, steadfastness, will to be emancipated, devotion, conscience, despair, renunciation etc. The level of intelligence is revealed in the light of wisdom and discrimination. This is the world of form, taste, sound, smell and touch. The world of intuition enters after wisdom — its attributes are clairvoyance and truth realisation. *Iksha* is above all these. It means creation and pursuit as well. But the chaotic work of the above bureaucrats we see the manifestation of this *Iksha* is delayed.

What is this chaos? When the mind influences the judgment of intellect, then the judgment is not pure, or when the urge of vital interferes with the feeling of the mind— the chaos sets in. The work of *Prana* or vital will do its own job, mind should not interfere. The mind will do its work where the influence of intellect is not at all preferable. Whenever two or more senses become involved - only desires, weaknesses, false fears come into play.

This is nothing but chaos and is not desirable as it becomes a hindrance to manifestation of being.

If all senses act as per their scheduled functions, then mortification comes first. Later comes non-attachment. When all these bureaucrats function as per the determined schedule, we will understand that the work of *Iksha* is complete. Then we can realise the existence and power of *Iksha*. What we can't do in our whole of our life it can happen in the blink of an eye.

The realm of this entity will be governed in the right way. As we shall neither shrink in response to the outer world, nor shall we be excited either. Reactions aroused by the external events should be accepted very quietly by means of the organised senses and feelings and finally all will be presented before the deliberations of *Iksha*. We shall act according to the verdict of *Iksha*. Then and then only we can follow the path of real surrender.

VAULT OF HEAVEN

Let us now leave the inner world to have a look into the outer world. We find planets and stars in the night sky, a familiar scene from our childhood. Let's look at something in the sky which is closest to us - the Moon, Earth's satellite. Shining but not twinkling as it is not a star. No matter how much it shines, its brilliance is borrowed from the Sun. Sunlight is reflected on the surface of the moon and so we can see our nearest neighbour.

The full moon, new moon, lunar eclipse and solar eclipse happen due to different positions of these three viz. Sun, Earth and Moon. Gravitational force of the Moon causes tidal waves in seas on Earth. The earth revolves around the sun and also revolves around its axis but the moon revolves around the earth but does not revolve around its own axis and as a result we can never see the other side of the moon while we are on earth. Since the moon is only the nearest celestial object to earth we give importance to the moon. It is 2,40,250 miles away from earth.

The Sun is 9,30,00,000 miles from Earth. The Earth revolves around the Sun at a speed of 30 kM per second. This means 67,000 miles per hour. The length of this orbit of the earth around the Sun is 58,69,20,000 miles.

The world of ours takes about 24 hours to rotate completely on its axis. We call it a day. The earth revolves around the Sun in about 365 days. We call this a year. Not only the planet earth but we also travel so many miles in space every year.

This Earth is the third planet of the sun. The Sun's nearest planet is Mercury. It takes three earth-months to orbit the sun. Then comes Venus, it takes a little over seven earth-months to complete orbiting. Then Mars, which takes 1.9 Earth-years to orbit the Sun. In between Earth and Mars there is the Asteroid Belt - full of small and large objects. They also revolve around the sun. So far, these planets form the inner Solar system. The Earth is the biggest among them.

After them is the planet Jupiter. Its volume is so big that it can hold 1,300 earths in its belly. One year of Jupiter is equivalent to 12 earth years. It has about 80 moons or satellites.

Strange worlds have been found on these satellites. Lava ejected from very high volcanos on such satellites cannot overcome the gravitational force of Jupiter to come back to the satellite itself. They make a continuous ring between Jupiter and the said satellites by accumulation of ejected matter. By observing the critical mass, volume of Jupiter and other properties scientists have come to the conclusion that Jupiter has nearly missed being considered as a star for few shortcomings. The force of gravitation in its core is so strong that the scientists assume that by this huge pressure and temperature the core has turned Carbon into a huge diamond which is often found within a star in Nova state. I shall discuss this Nova in due course.

Then comes Saturn orbiting the Sun. It takes 30 earth-years to complete the orbit. Its moons or satellites are 83 in number. Seven rings composed of various comets, asteroids, dust particles covered with ice are rotating in a circle. Jupiter also has several such rings. Saturn is 772 times bigger compared to earth in size.

Then comes Uranus with its 27 satellites. It is 56 times the size of the earth. It takes 84 Earth years to orbit the Sun.

Then Neptune. It takes 165 Earth years to orbit the sun. It is 59 times bigger than the earth in size. It has 14 satellites.

Then Pluto, it takes 248 Earth years to revolve around the Sun. Its volume is one-tenth of that of the Earth. It has 5 satellites. Recently, astronomers are refusing to consider Pluto as a planet.

After the Earth, the planets up to this point are called the Outer Solar System.

Apart from these nine planets, a study about the tenth planet is going on and its existence with the help of mathematics has been proven. The planet is estimated to be about the same size as Neptune.

But its orbit is different from that of Pluto. It has been named Planet X.

GALAXIES

This far is our solar system. Sun is also in this family. But it is not stationary. It is also orbiting along with its family around an arm of Orion constellation of our Milky Way Galaxy with a speed is 9,00,000 miles per hour. At the same time, we are alsorunning in space riding on earth.

The length of the orbit of the most distant planet Pluto, is 483,82,44,000 miles. To cover this distance, light takes about 7.2 hours. Velocity of light is 186,000 miles per second.

Our brain has to negotiate this distance with its limited world of measurements with meters, feet, yards, miles etc. With a calm mind if we start thinking we shall have the idea of expanse of this vast space of the solar system where we live.

This is the volume of the solar system that is discovered till date. Then the outer space where there are innumerable constellations lying like islands on the sea of space. To visit one island to another island Light with its speed of 1,86,000 miles per second takes thousands of years.

Let us discuss the Galaxy where our solar system belongs to. It is called the Milky Way in English. It is said in Greek mythology that milk from Greek goddess Hero's breast spilled in that region and so is the name.

In Sanskrit it is called *Chayapath* , more mysterious allusion - the path which the Gods select to pass through.

Whatever the name is, we call it the Milky Way Galaxy. There are many such galaxies in this Universe. In the Milky Way Galaxy, numerous suns, stars and their gaseous progenitors exist. All these substances are moving spirally. All known galaxies have a supermassive black hole at the centre of mass of the galaxy. Their details are still not known fully or exactly. But something is there, one which cannot be seen, but these impossible masses of revolving constellations is rotating around this unknown object.

This Galaxy is like a spinning wheel. Earlier it was thought that the Sun was in its centre. But later this idea was proven to be wrong. We are in an arm of this galactic system called Orion Arm. This arm's length is 2,000 light years. Our Milky Way Galaxy is 50,000 light years in length. It takes the Sun 20 billion earth years to make a complete rotation around the Centre. The speed of the Sun is 138 miles per second. Now, fix the mind a little on the length of this orbit! Immeasurable numbers of such galaxies are scattered in this vast outer space. They are moving away at unimaginable speeds from each other.

Now we shall try to understand the universe described in the next chapters.

NATURE OF UNIVERSE

Quasars, Black Holes & Curvature of space

When the star gazers look into the sky to find a new star, they are actually looking into the past. The further away the star is the more they go into the past. Matter of fact distant stars are millions of light years away from us. Time taken for the light to reach us is a million years . God knows in these millions of years whether the star is present or it is disintegrated through the process of natural destruction. The root cause is the distance. We are looking at their past formation. Even the first light of the day from our Sun takes 8 minutes to reach the earth. We find the Sun after it has risen 8 minutes earlier.

Their past is seen by us as present. One day it may happen that we shall fail to find them as these celestial objects are no longer existing in present time. This event occurs very often. I shall try to throw some light on the space time continuum factor.

At present let us concentrate upon our position in the observable Universe.

460,000,000,000 or 4.6 billion years ago about the ⅓ of the life of this visible universe, huge gas and aggregates of gas and dust are concentrated to create enormous temperature and pressure. A medium sized star, that is our Sun was born under this great pressure and temperature.

Various matters around the newborn Sun, when cooled down, took part in forming this solar system.

In the future when this middle-aged Sun would exhaust its hydrogen fuel it would turn into a heat station, and in course of time it would become a Red Giant and it would bulge out, rising beyond the orbits of Mercury, Venus and Earth, to finally devour them in its molten mass of hell.

If we take a look we can observe twenty suns around the Sun of our solar system.

Their names are as follows:

Alpha Centauri, Barnard's Star, Sirius, Epsilon Eridani, Ross 154, Procyon, Wolf 359, Luyten 726-B, Luyten 725-32, for Lacaille 9352 Epsilon Indi, Tau Ceti, Lalande 21185, 61 Cygni, Ross 248, Groombridge 34 Struve 2398, Giclass 51-15, Luyten 789-6, Luyten 726-8.

Imagine them in a tube or cylinder. Its diameter will be 20 light years, that is = 20x 365x24x60x60x3,00,000 KM

= 1892,16,000,000,000 KM

Our sun is a typical yellow coloured star. Neighbouring star Proxima Centauri (part of a triple star system of Alpha Centauri) is the closest star to the Sun at 4.2465 light-years away. It takes time for sunlight to reach 4.3 light years (speed of light is 1,86,000 miles per second).

Most of the stars are paired or triple and may have planets. There are also singles, like our Sun. It is possible that Barnard's star, which is 6 light years away, may have a planet, the size of which is close to that of Jupiter.

Next, we have to go to the Milky Way Galaxy. Before 1920 this galaxy was thought to be our universe. But today we know that in this universe there are billions of Galaxies like the Milky Way Galaxy. There are billions of stars and vast constellations revolve endlessly.

Some of them are very old which are reddish in nature. The spiral arm of galaxies is simply full of gas and aggregates of dust particles and every now and then new stars are created.

Beyond the limits of this Milky Way Galaxy, we can find at least 20 Galaxies where our Milky Way Galaxy belongs to. These are called Local Groups.

While determining the nature of the universe astronomer Allan Sandage says, "Galaxies in astronomy are as similar as molecules in physics."

Our Milky Way galaxy and its companion Andromeda Galaxy M31 and a smaller one named M33 Galaxy - all three are spiraling round and round at very high speed. Hundreds of Star clusters and dust clouds are present in the Andromeda Galaxy. Earlier mistakenly it was thought to be Nebula or Cloud of nebula of the Milky Way Galaxy.

NGC (New Galactic Chart) 205 is an Elliptical Galaxy crowded with old stars. Large & Small Magellanic Clouds are thought to be irregular galaxies as this galaxy seems to be spinning at its own will, but further investigations showed that as a result of their mutual attraction, they are locked to each other in spite of the very high rate of expansion of the universe. These 20 galaxies are:

Milky Way, Leo I & Ii, Ursa Minor, Draco, Sculptor, Small & Large Magellanic Cloud, Formax, Carina, IC 1613, M33, Andromeda, M 31, M32, NGC 205, NGC 185, And I, II & III, NGC 147. They spread around 200,000 light years across the universe. This Local Group is like a flock of ships which belong to Supercluster. The range is approximately 75,000,000 light years across.

Virgo is a very rich constellation — its position is about 50,000,000 light years away from the Local Group, which is very near to the centre of the Local Supercluster. Research on Superclusters reveals sensational information. Endless space lies between two superclusters. Some astronomers think that this universe is like a big sponge and in between spaces are connected with fine veins or Thin Filament like things. Astronomers started determining the density of matter present in these star rich areas to determine the density of matter present in this universe. If this density of matter is found to be minimum or same as a certain quantity, the universe will disappear forever due to expansion. If the density is more than a certain quantity, the expansion will stop and the universal contraction will set in. The location of this supercluster is between the billions of Superclusters and the Quasar. If we look into deep space, we see all these Superclusters, Quasar, and the Galaxies, they are moving away from each other with unimaginable speed. On the visible cosmic horizon, we can see innumerable Quasars or Quasi Stellar objects, and one more mind-boggling event - isotropic radiation of the Big Bang, the creation of this universe. This universe has no centre, any observer finds the universe the same from any location. This universe is ISOTROPIC, which means it looks the same from any location. Quasar is the most distant object in the universe. The attached picture (image 2) is the artist's impression where the accretion disc is rendered in ULAS J1120+0641, a very distant quasar powered by a supermassive black hole with a mass of two billion times.

Image2

Now of course the Galaxy Candidate HD1 is the most distant cosmic object. Its distance is approximately 1,350,000,000 light years. Below is the picture given (Image 3). The first galaxy is 100 million years from the beginning of the Big Bang event.   Image 3

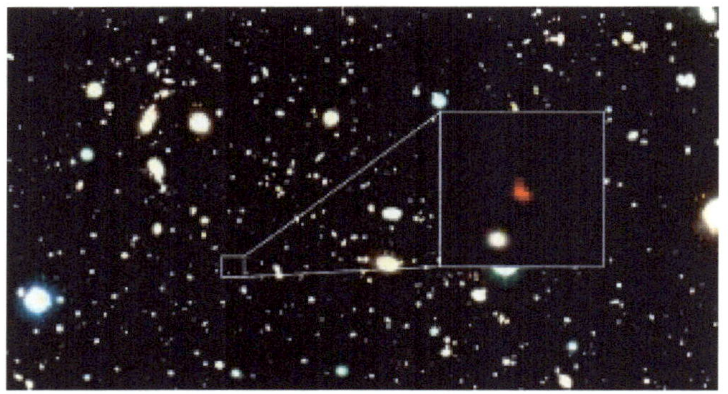

However, Quasar is very mysterious object and also a reservoir of infinite energy and radiance.

Quasars, much smaller than the Milky Way galaxy in size, are able to radiate more than the combined energy of hundreds of our Galaxy.

The most distant cosmic objects are moving away from us at 90 percent of the speed of light. Their light takes billions of years to come to us. By this time there must have been more changes in them, but there is no way to know that. Simulation on a computer is the method by which scientists are relentlessly trying to find out the truth. Finding it means that we shall be looking into the past scenario of billions of years ago, even during the formation of the universe billions of years ago.

For the tireless work of modern astronomers this novel invention was made and it is possible to witness the event. One galaxy was found to spray continual mass of matter and spread into space. That mass is approximately equal to five light years or 5x186000x60x60x24x365 miles or 29,328,480,000,000 miles. This is only a part of the massive material flow. That Galaxy is a special Galaxy. So that the first recognized Quasar 3C 48 and 3C 273 can be found.

QUASARS, BLACK HOLES, CURVATURE OF SPACE

The first Quasar was discovered in 1960 since then the whole of astronomical society have been stunned to observe the nature of Quasars. They seem to be a single point of light at an infinite distance moving away from us with unimaginable speed yet they radiate thousand times more light emitting subatomic particles than what a galaxy is able to do.

To measure the dispersed energy of a Quasar first let us consider a large nuclear powered electricity generation plant capable of producing 1,000 megawatts of electricity. Now multiply this by 10^{31} to get the magnitude of the dissipated energy of the quasar.

Space scientists say the turbulent Galaxies harbour these quasars at their core More than a million quasars have been discovered till date. The nearest one is around 600 million light years away from us.

Image.. 4

Many scientists think that at one quarter of the span of the current age of the universe, Quasars came into being. Since then, they are moving away from us at tremendous speed; maybe those we see today have become extinct due to continuous radiation of energy.

Where is the source of quasar's energy? Out of various doctrines it is found probable that this source is located at the heart of the Galaxy.

The idea is that there is a superheated rotating accretion disk which is the cause of rotation of the gaseous material flowing in its trap and finally increases the momentum of the vast material objects to eject them into the universe nearly with the speed of light.

The diameter of this wheel is estimated to be the same as three times the distance from Earth to Pluto and that mysterious core harbours a giant spiral which is called a Black Hole.

Reason is given below, from which we can understand why the above object is called black hole. To prove their existence is almost impossible. When substance or Matter is brought to reach its extremely condensed state, black hole is created, of course there are some preconditions. Suppose our earth is condensed to the size of a marble - it could become a black hole. When matter is concentrated to its extreme state, the gravitational force becomes so strong that no object including rays of light can escape from its attraction. Even the diffused light returns to it again. Gravitational confinement of light rays does not allow radiated light to come out from it and the light rays become invisible as they cannot reach the eyes of observers. So, the object disappears in space. One more event occurs - as a result of its unusual attraction the fabric of space around is curved creating a self-created abyss and its visibility is lost from the universe.

This unimaginably large gravitational force acts strangely enough with space and time. According to Sir Albert Einstein time is a dimensional element like length, width etc. At present I am at a certain point in space time continuum. But there is a future or a past somewhere else. Let's suppose I'm in this black hole or have fallen into a black hole. If I turn my head, I shall find all the future activities and happenings of the entire universe one after another. But the observer outside this gravitational attraction would find that it takes eternity to cross the boundary of the black hole.

Black holes are of roughly three sizes. Experts say in next instant of Big Bang (Conventional idea about creation of the universe) the super-concentrated part broke down and created a number of very small black holes. Expansion was going on in the rest of the universe. The diameters of these black holes were as tiny as the nucleus of an atom but its masses were billions of tons. It is assumed that they were destroyed long ago after the explosion but some may still remain and for which we find occasional violent explosions in this space.

A medium-sized black hole is formed when an enormously big star is destroyed it becomes a Neutron Star and eventually lives in captivity.

Image 5

A Neutron Star is a twin star. If it draws matter from its partner's body the system crosses the certain limit of mass and is transformed into a medium-sized black hole. Pulsar Stars combine in a 3 billion years' gap and finally this type of Black Hole is created.

Image 6   Pulsar star

PULSAR STAR

But it is assumed that the giant black holes may exist in the centre of the galaxy created during the early formation of the galaxy. By the vortex pull due to gravity, the matter is drawn towards the centre and Black Hole is created. Black Hole in NGC 4151 Galaxy has mass equal to the mass of 10 billion suns, but its diameter is only three quarters of the distance between Earth and Jupiter.

Image 7   NGC 4151 Galaxy below.

NGC 4152

Constellations are the food of Black Holes. The stars come and fall into them because of their strong pull. By exhausting themselves they disintegrate into fountains of endless energy and light. This is a novel way of generating energy. Quasars are now thought to be the state of transition through which the Galaxies were passing, and at the same time the black holes inside them were devouring the stars and gaseous matter by the force of gravitation.

When the universe was at ¼ of its current size, collisions of stars used to happen due to tremendous contraction in space and they turned their fellow celestial bodies to their own food. So, for these quasars there was probably no shortage of food. These quasars had run out of time. Apparently in the meantime most of the Galaxies had run out of their fuel near their centres. The above said quasars waited patiently for their prey. Now and often, there are signs of star devourer.

Image 8.......Image of Centaurus A

CENTAURUS A

A mysterious black band has been noted in the heart of the turbulent core of Centaurus A galaxy. It is thought that this Cen A, on dismembering another old and bigger galaxy had been supplying the remaining parts to the central black monster of Cen Ab as it's food.

Now the question is : Is there any such monster sleeping in our Milky Way galaxy? Radio Astronomers have found one unusual black spot in the centre of our galaxy. It may be a black hole. The presence of Supermassive Black Hole named Sagittarius A* is assumed in our Galaxy.

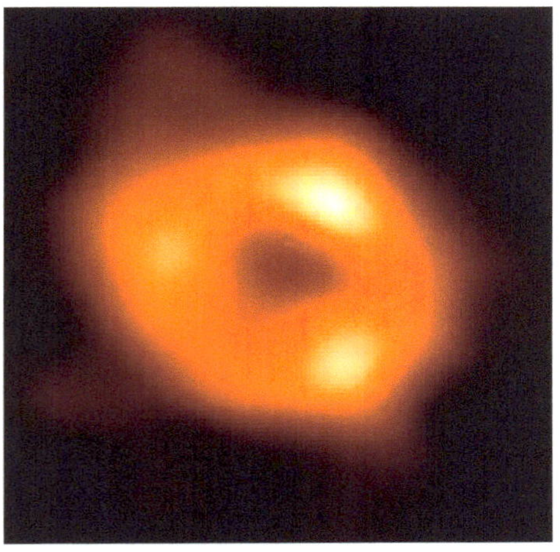

IMAGE 9.   SAGITTARIUS A*

BIRTH AND DEATH OF STARS

"Among the celestial objects where my mind is wandering far and farthest in waking or dormant state, now may it enter into state of benevolent volition" —*Yajurveda*

This living planet of ours with all its continents, oceans, animal kingdom all are made out of sacrifice of a distant star. Though Hydrogen and Helium were created as a result of the Big Bang but the complex atomic and subatomic particles with which this world and its inhabitants are built, their birth is the result of destruction of the body parts of the dying passerby star. Arms of the Spiral Galaxy are rich in stellar debris with accompanying gaseous clouds and dust — which is called the birthplace of the new star. When the arms of a galaxy are thus gradually stressed, the stellar objects gather round their centres by their own gravitational force. When these masses become enough, they give rise to new stars. If these concentrated masses happen to be less to 1/10th of the mass of our sun then they are called 'Brown Dwarf. Vide next page for image 10.

Image 10...................Image of BROWN DWARF

The planet Jupiter of the solar system is this type of object. Due to insufficient mass, no nuclear fission took place. Still, it is radiating heat. Our Sun god or any such star of equivalent size or mass has its own history. They remained as Nebula, rich in gas and dust particles at the beginning of creation. When a sufficient amount of substance becomes concentrated, the centre part implodes and stars are created.

Then a radiation storm of particles continues in this particular situation. Then Helium originates from

Hydrogen. Our Sun is 4.6 billion years old, and it is in the middle of its life.

When Hydrogen finishes its storage because they added themselves together to become Helium. Now in the centre, contractions still continue resulting in combustion. But the external shell continues to expand and in this state the star is Called Red Giant. Image 11.

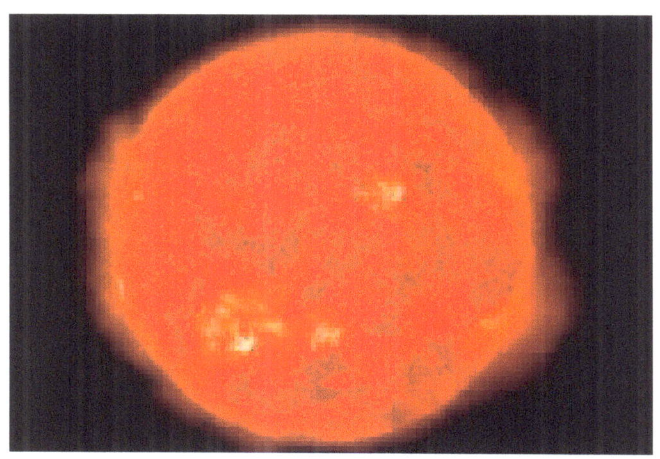

Image 11. .Image of RED GIANT

Its interior is now filled with pure helium surrounded by molten layer of Hydrogen. With more compression Helium starts to fuse in the heat resulting energy radiation. This goes on for thousands of years. Finally, Helium is converted to Carbon — which is a steady state. The outer layer vanishes slowly into the surrounding space leaving a steady state. Then the centre is called White Dwarf which cools down slowly. Image 12 below:

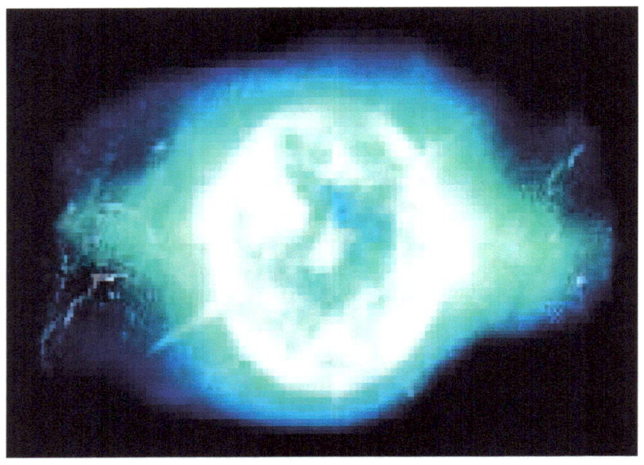

Image 12   Image of WHITE DWARF

Remember the words of a poet "Like a diamond in the sky" - maybe a huge diamond will turn into a chunk in the core.

Stars that are ten times the mass of our sun started their lives in the same process but for their heavy mass their last days begin too early. Helium at their core turns into Carbon and subsequently turns into

Iron which does not radiate, on the contrary it absorbs energy.

For this reason, tremendous pressure is generated at the centre due to gravitational force. It sends very high shock waves that are transmitted outward. Due to this shock a very high temperature is generated and finally the whole system explodes with the brilliance of hundreds of thousand suns resulting in Supernova.

Image 13.   IMAGE OF SUPERNOVA

Caught in LMC in March-April 1987. It is filled with subatomic particles called Neutrons.

Speed of rotation of skating players increases on ice while they fold their outstretched arms to their chest. Similarly, here also due to the pull of gravity when substances are collected at the centre the rotation increases. This increases the power of the magnetic field to a tune of a billion times. Dispersion of charged subatomic particles near this field keeps happening. This was called Pulsar Star or pulsating star. The system sends radio and other waves at fixed time intervals.

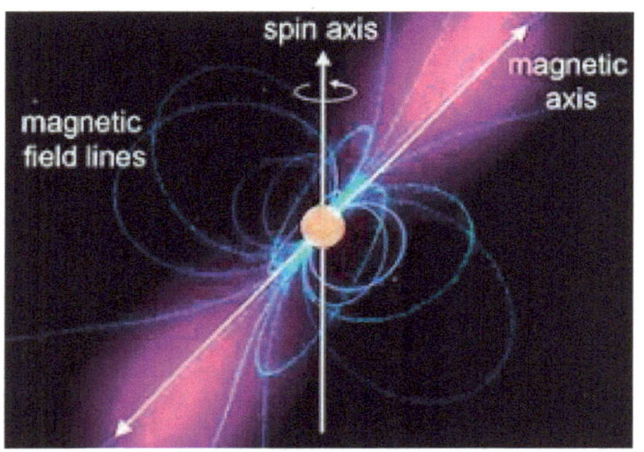

Image14   PULSAR STAR

They act like a lighthouse in space. Life span of stars which are thirty or fifty times the mass of the Sun is comparatively less. When they run out of fuel its heat fails to hold out the star with its own gravity forces it to collapse. Then it turns into our familiar Black Hole and subsequently gets Lost in self-created eternal space.

BIRTH OF UNIVERSE & DETERMINATION OF TIME

Dakshinamurthy stotram

बीजस्याऽन्तरिवाङ्कुरो जगदिदं प्राङ्गनिर्विकल्पंपुनः

मायाकल्पितदेशकालकलना वैचित्र्यचित्रीकृतम् ।

मायावीव विजृम्भयत्यपि महायोगीव यः स्वेच्छया

तस्मै श्रीगुरुमूर्तये नम इदं श्रीदक्षिणामूर्तये ॥२॥

By Srimad Shankaracharya.

Transliteration

Biijasya-Antar-Iva-Angkuro Jagad[t]-Idam Praangga-Nirvikalpam Punah

Maayaa-Kalpita-Desha-Kaala-Kalanaa Vaicitrya-Citrii-Krtam |

Maayaavi-Iva Vijrmbhayaty-Api
Mahaa-Yogi-Iva Yah Sve[a-I]cchayaa

Tasmai Shrii-Guru-Muurtaye Nama Idam
Shrii-Dakssinnaamuurtaye ||2||

Meaning

To him, like a magician or even like a great Yogin, displays, by His own will, this universe which at the beginning is undifferentiated like the sprout in the seed, but which is made again Differentiated under the varied conditions of space and time posited by *māyā*. To Him, of the form of the Preceptor, the blessed *Dakshinamurti* may this obeisance be!

The above is just like the statement of modern physics. According to scientists when the age of the universe was almost zero means at (10^{-43} seconds), then its volume was only 10^{-28} cm i.e. many times smaller than the Hydrogen atom. All visible and invisible matter is within it but wrapped in the form of a seed. It is the same condition for space and time. There was no space, so time was also absent. Although the size was almost zero, the mass was immense. Then we get the great explosion called the Big Bang, for which the expansion of the universe began. Since then the universe is expanding, the great celestial objects are moving apart from themselves at tremendous speed. More the distance from us, the more is the speed, reaching almost the speed of light.

Image 15 Expansion after Big Bang

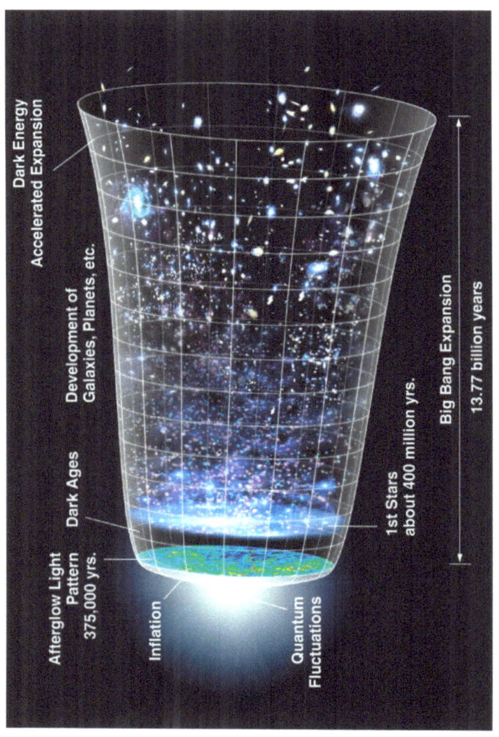

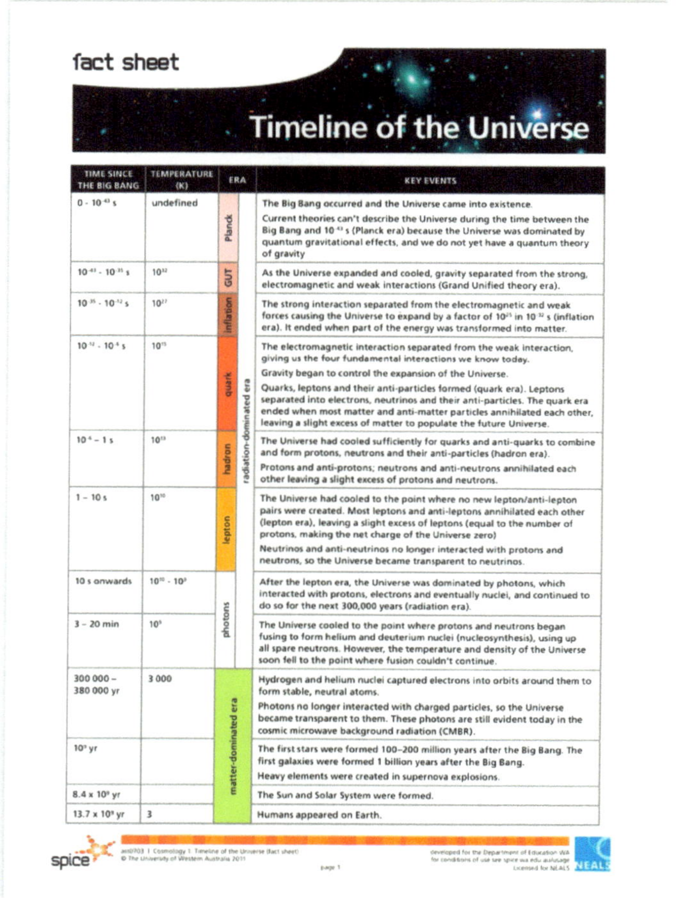

TIME SINCE THE BIG BANG	TEMPERATURE (K)	ERA	KEY EVENTS
$0 - 10^{-43}$ s	undefined	Planck	The Big Bang occurred and the Universe came into existence. Current theories can't describe the Universe during the time between the Big Bang and 10^{-43} s (Planck era) because the Universe was dominated by quantum gravitational effects, and we do not yet have a quantum theory of gravity
$10^{-43} - 10^{-35}$ s	10^{32}	GUT	As the Universe expanded and cooled, gravity separated from the strong, electromagnetic and weak interactions (Grand Unified theory era).
$10^{-35} - 10^{-12}$ s	10^{27}	inflation	The strong interaction separated from the electromagnetic and weak forces causing the Universe to expand by a factor of 10^{25} in 10^{-32} s (inflation era). It ended when part of the energy was transformed into matter.
$10^{-12} - 10^{-6}$ s	10^{15}	quark	The electromagnetic interaction separated from the weak interaction, giving us the four fundamental interactions we know today. Gravity began to control the expansion of the Universe. Quarks, leptons and their anti-particles formed (quark era). Leptons separated into electrons, neutrinos and their anti-particles. The quark era ended when most matter and anti-matter particles annihilated each other, leaving a slight excess of matter to populate the future Universe.
$10^{-6} - 1$ s	10^{13}	hadron	The Universe had cooled sufficiently for quarks and anti-quarks to combine and form protons, neutrons and their anti-particles (hadron era). Protons and anti-protons; neutrons and anti-neutrons annihilated each other leaving a slight excess of protons and neutrons.
$1 - 10$ s	10^{10}	lepton	The Universe had cooled to the point where no new lepton/anti-lepton pairs were created. Most leptons and anti-leptons annihilated each other (lepton era), leaving a slight excess of leptons (equal to the number of protons, making the net charge of the Universe zero) Neutrinos and anti-neutrinos no longer interacted with protons and neutrons, so the Universe became transparent to neutrinos.
10 s onwards	$10^{10} - 10^{9}$	photons	After the lepton era, the Universe was dominated by photons, which interacted with protons, electrons and eventually nuclei, and continued to do so for the next 300,000 years (radiation era).
$3 - 20$ min	10^{9}		The Universe cooled to the point where protons and neutrons began fusing to form helium and deuterium nuclei (nucleosynthesis), using up all spare neutrons. However, the temperature and density of the Universe soon fell to the point where fusion couldn't continue.
$300\,000 - 380\,000$ yr	$3\,000$	matter-dominated era	Hydrogen and helium nuclei captured electrons into orbits around them to form stable, neutral atoms. Photons no longer interacted with charged particles, so the Universe became transparent to them. These photons are still evident today in the cosmic microwave background radiation (CMBR).
10^{9} yr			The first stars were formed 100–200 million years after the Big Bang. The first galaxies were formed 1 billion years after the Big Bang. Heavy elements were created in supernova explosions.
8.4×10^{9} yr			The Sun and Solar System were formed.
13.7×10^{9} yr	3		Humans appeared on Earth.

Timeline of Universe

Almost from zero universe time still it is expanding and gradually all the elements emerged.

Today's physicists determined those times. There was no space or time and after then space came into being as a result of expansion and then came the time too.

The question is what was there before??

Few millennia ago this wisdom was revealed in *Rik Veda* by the sages and seers of ancient India.

नासदीय सुक्तम् Nasadiya Suktam - Ṛik Veda

Perhaps no other Vedic Hymn equals in depth and majesty of this famous Hymn of Creation known to tradition as the *Nāsādiya Sukta* (Not the non-existent) from its opening words. Its seer, Prajāpati Parameshthin, Supreme Lord of Creatures, chants in the "triple-praise" meter his knowledge and his wonder as he recalls his vision and in these seven immortal mantras - seven like the days of creation- plants seeds of Vedic metaphysics and mathematics. For this hymn, besides being a cosmogony, is also a beautiful meditation on the properties of numbers from one to nine and zero. Thus, creation begins in the Absolute, the one without a second. "Where neither nonbeing nor being was as yet". Then the duality creeps in, darkness conceals darkness. And so, it all begins.

नासदासीन्नो सदासीत्तदानींनासीद्रजो नो व्योमा परो
यत् किमावरीवः कुह कस्य शर्मन्नम्भःकिमासीद्ग
गहना गभीरम् ॥१॥

nā́sad āsīn nó sád āsīt tadā́nīṃ

nā́sīd rájo nó víoma paró yát

kím ā́varīvaḥ kúha kásya śármann

ámbhaḥ kím āsīd gáhanaṃ gabhīrám ..1

Then even non-existence was not there, nor existence, There was no air then, nor the space beyond it. What covered it? Where was it? In whose keeping? Was there then cosmic fluid, in depths unfathomed?..1

न मृत्युरासीदमृतं न तर्हि न रात्र्या अह्नआसीत्प्रकेतः |
आनीदवातं स्वधया तदेकंतस्माद्धान्यन्न परः
किञ्चनास ॥२॥

ná mṛtyúr āsīd amṛ́taṃ ná tárhi

na rā́triyā áhna āsīt praketáḥ

ā́nīd avātáṃ svadháyā tád ékaṃ

tásmād dhānyán ná paráḥ kím canā́sa ..2

Then there was neither death nor immortality
nor was there then the torch of night and day.
The One breathed windlessly and self-sustaining.
There was that One then, and there was no other ..2

तम आसीत्तमसा गूढ़मग्रेऽप्रकेतंसलिलं सर्वमा इदम् |

तुच्छ्येनाभ्वपिहितंयदासीत्तपसस्तन्महिनाजायतैकम्
|| ३ ||

táma āsīt támasā gūhram ágre

apraketám salilám sárvam ā idám

atuchyénābhú ápihitaṃ yád ásīt

tápasas tán mahinájāyataíkam

At first there was only darkness wrapped in darkness. All this was only unillumined cosmic water. That One which came to be, enclosed in nothing, arose at last, born of the power of knowledge..3

कामस्तदग्रे समवर्तताधि मनसो रेतः प्रथमं यदासीत् |

सतो बन्धुमसति निरविन्दन्हृदि प्रतीष्या कवयो मनीषा
|| ४ ||

kā́mas tád ágre sám avartatā́dhi

mánaso rétaḥ prathamáṃ yád ā́sīt

sató bándhum ásati nír avindan

hṛdí pratī́ṣyā kaváyo manīṣā́ ..4

In the beginning desire descended on it that was the primal seed, born of the mind.The sages who have searched their hearts with wisdom know that which is, is kin to that which is not..4

तिरश्चीनो विततो रश्मिरेषामध:स्विदासीदुपरि स्विदासीत् ।

रेतोधा आसन्महिमान आसन् स्वधाअवस्तात्प्रयतिः परस्तात् ॥५॥

tiraścíno vítato raśmír eṣām

Radháḥ svid āsī́d upári svid āsīt

retodhā́ āsan mahimā́na āsan

svadhā́ avástāt práyatiḥ parástat ..5

Seminal powers made fertile mighty forces.
Below was strength, and over it was impulse..5

को अद्धा वेद क इह प्रवोचत्कुतआजाता कुत इयं
विसृष्टिः

अर्वाग्देवा अस्य विसर्जनेनाथा कोवेद यत आबभूव ॥६॥

kó addhā́ veda ká ihá prá vocat

kúta ā́jātā kúta iyáṃ vísṛṣṭiḥ

arvā́g devā́ asyá visárjanena

áthā kó veda yáta ābabhū́va ..6

But, after all, who knows, and who can say
Whence it all came, and how creation happened?
The gods themselves are later than creation,
So who knows truly whence it has arisen? ..6

इयं विसृष्टिर्यत आबभूव यदि वा दधेयदि वा न |

यो अस्याध्यक्षः परमे व्योमन्त्सोअङ्ग वेद यदि वा न वेद
॥७॥

iyáṃ vísṛṣṭir yáta ābabhū́va

yádi vā dadhé yádi vā ná

yó asyā́dhyakṣaḥ paramé vyoman

só aṅgá veda yádi vā ná véda ..7

Whence all creation had its origin,nthe creator,
whether he fashioned it or whether he did not,the

creator, who surveys it all from highest heaven,he knows — or maybe even he does not know..7

This seems to be the expression of the most modern physicists. Pressure of differentiated (*Ṛta* or dynamic) and undifferentiated (*Satya* or absolute static) Truth are responsible for expansion of the seed like universe to reach the emergence of *Prana* (Life Force). Then step by step came different developments of the same form.

Then Maya (illusive truth) and the space came into being. All visible and apparent invisible things are created by illusory play of time and space. A spark was needed to make this successful as an observable universe. Then Life force or *Prana* emerged from matter due to pressure of vital.

With the universal evolution of everything which was involved as a seed form with the pre cataclysmic hysteresis it was inevitable to come out as a visible and invisible universe. Creation has no end and no beginning.

But where is the urge coming from?

It must have been hidden in the seed form, the cause of which is more subtle things. Causal form of Life or *Prana* is part of *Parachaitanya* or Super consciousness. The *Prana* comes directly from It.

Now the existence of the entire and overall forms of consciousness is nothing but *Brahma*-consciousness. In it the billion universes are not the last word, because existential consciousness is *Nirvikalpa* (Absolute / unerring) there.

All space, time and creation are inseparable. There is neither inside nor outside. All is consciousness or *Chaitanya*. Consciousness is its repository. Consciousness is its manifestation. Consciousness is its Existence and existence is its consciousness. Seed of the dispersion of Infinite number universes and cause of the deluge set in with pre creative volition.

The power behind the creation of the universe and the incredible force that causes matter to take different forms pose puzzling questions to our Astrophysicists. They are creating substances which in turn create substances of our daily use. In this process tremendous flow of energy and flare of effulgence become visible. At this stage the supreme being is *Viswattirna* **(Transcendental).** When He set up innate relationship between the universe and hearts of every element of earth He is termed as *Viswatmak* **(global).**

A FEW LATEST IMAGES FROM NASA

5 latest images of supernova, stars, and others captured by NASA James Webb Space Telescope

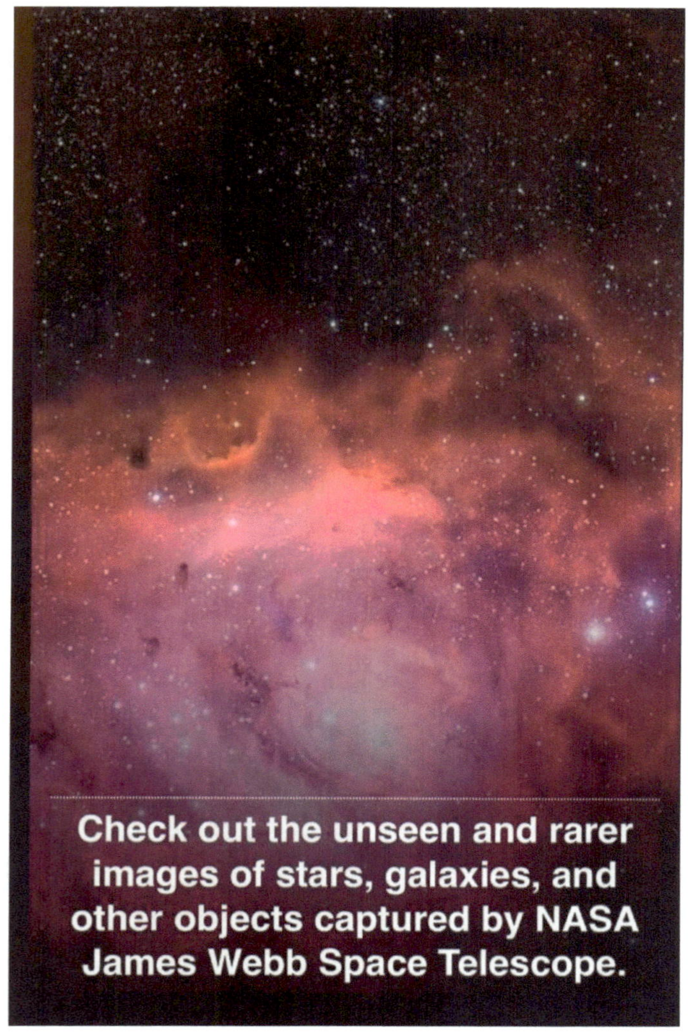

Check out the unseen and rarer
images of stars, galaxies, and
other objects captured by NASA
James Webb Space Telescope.

NASA's James Webb Space Telescope
reveals the Rho Ophiuchi cloud
complex, the closest star-forming region
to Earth on July 12, 2023 in space.

NGC 346, shown here in this image from NASA's James Webb Space Telescope Near-Infrared Camera (NIRCam), is a dynamic star cluster that lies within a nebula 200,000 light years away.

The Pillars of Creation that are set off in a
kaleidoscope of color in NASAs James Webb Space
Telescopes near-infrared-light view in this handout
photo provided by NASA on Oct. 19, 2022.

Shells of cosmic dust created by the
interaction of binary stars appear like
tree rings around Wolf-Rayet 140.

NASA uses advanced telescopes and
instruments to study the composition
and structure of nebulae.

Nebulae are vast clouds of dust and gas
in space. They are often regions where
new stars are born.

NASA's Hubble Space Telescope has captured stunning images of various nebulae. It can be found throughout the Milky Way galaxy and beyond.

NASA's James Webb Space Telescope reveals the Rho Ophiuchi cloud complex, the closest star-forming region to Earth on July 12, 2023 in space.

EPILOGUE

The yogis and sages of India long ago felt that the outer world is only a projection of the inner world. Therefore, they have revealed the wealth of their Sadhana in scriptures - but since the process of Sadhana (disciplined and dedicated esoteric practices for pursuit of self realisation), is very much esoteric in nature, they took the help of metaphors to expose the outlines of the pursuit.

It seems that all things are different from each other but they realised that the final constituent of all things is one and the same. Lack of life in living beings is known as death. In search of the source of Life force or *PRANA*, they wanted to transcend the state of restless *PRANA* (which may be termed as Mind) to know from where life originates - only then it is possible to bring life under control. The text below sheds light on this matter.

Chetana (or consciousness) is one of the attributes of Prana (vital force). Chaitanya is cognitive consciousness. So, I feel the need to write something about Prana or life force.

The entire universe is made up of Five Great Elements – Earth (Khiti), Water (Ap), Fire (Tej), Air (Marut), Space (Byom).Each of them inextricably linked with each other – As in Khiti or Earth there is ½ part of Khiti and the rest consists of ⅛ the part of each remaining four. In *AP* or water there is ½ part of *Ap* and the rest consists of ⅛ the part of each of the remaining four. In *Tej* or *Fire* there is ½ part of *Tej*and the rest consists of ⅛ the part of each of the remaining four. In *Marut* or air there is ½ part of *Marut* and the rest consists of ⅛ the part of each of the remaining four, in *Byom* or space there is ½ part of *Byom* and ⅛ th the part of each of the remaining four. So-called science has not progressed much with regard to *Prana* or Life force.

What is the relationship between the things written below with *Prana* or Life Force?

1. Mind, intellect, Chitta (conscious vital elements), Ahamkar (Idea of separate identity)

2. Khiti (Earth), Ap (Water), Tej (Fire), Marut (Air), Byom (Space).

3. Eyes, ears, nose, tongue, skin

4. Speech, hand, feet, anus, genital organ

5. Smell, touch, appearance, taste, sound

6. Space, Time

7. Atma (Self)

8. Iksha (Will)

9. Hatred, Lust, Anger, Greed, Infatuation, ego, Jealousy

I have tried to explain in my statement below.

Twenty-four ethos or principles :

Twenty-four ethos or Attributes spread like a spider's web inside us. Human acts sometimes as controller and some time as being controlled or possessed by them :

Khiti, Ap, Tej, Marut, Vyom 5

Eyes, ears, nose, tongue, skin 5

Speech, hands, feet, anus, genital.........5

Sound, touch, form, taste, smell 5

Mind, intellect, idea of separate

identity, unmanifest or nature..............4

—————-

Total   24

These are twenty-four ethos. They have merits, demerits too. Everything which is modest is virtue and excess is demerit. Instincts and other human responses - everyone knows the words like lust, desire, etc. connected with each tattva (ethos) and the subtle causes of each tattva. Each is the revealer of the other by the power of self-effulgent being in us and without which everything is useless and inert. Life force or *Prana*, consciousness, being conscious—all synonymous. Consciousness is instinctive but realisation of consciousness or cognitive consciousness is achieved by *Sadhana* (disciplined and dedicated esoteric practices) - which is called *Chaitanya* in Sanskrit.

The steps to achieve perfection in human life

* First ——— - Knowledge.

*Second——— Judgment, Discrimination

* Third ——— Adjustment, Balance

* Fourth —-— . Character

* Fifth——— Self-Control

* Sixth ———Clairvoyance

* Seventh -——- Concentration

* Eighth ——— -Intuition or Bodhi

* Ninth ———Ascension

* Tenth ———Realisation

* Eleventh———Analysis

*Twelfth ——— Awakening

* Thirteenth ——-Spiritual Feelings

* Fourteenth —— Understanding of identity

* Fifteenth ———Inner Perception

* Sixteenth —— Divine Qualities

* Seventeenth —- Determination. Volition

* Eighteenth ———-Superconsciousness

* Nineteenth———--Perfection

* Twentieth-——Revelation of Universal super consciousness or *Brahmajnan*

All this is at the centre of that spider's web where we are trying to reach. Until we get there, we are in domestic life. The spider makes the web with its own saliva. As if the observer is trying to understand the observer itself.

What about the power of the observer?

The distant visible universe is seen through the telescope. Image falls upside down on the ophthalmic organ of the observer. The size of the image is more or less like a point in the retina of the eye of the observer. Sensing the point image the observer sees the vast universe. It is nothing but the projection of the observer's mind.

Now when the observer turns his attention from outside into the inside of his being to realise the being itself, the real understanding or realisation can only be done through knowledge by identity. There is no other way to know oneself but to become one with oneself.

Now let's talk about death. What happens to these twenty-four tattvas or ethos after *jivatma* leaves the body during death.

Before that let's see what we can find in the ancient Scriptures :

There are three types of body:

I) **Gross Body** or *Sthuladeha* made of *Panchatattva* or Five great elements or ethos — *Khiti* (Earth), *Ap* (Water), *Tej* (Fire), *Marut* (Air), *Byom* (Space).

II) **Subtle body** or *Lingadeha* - consisting of Eighteenth Tattva -

i) Motor organs - *Vak*(speech), *Pani* (hands), *Pada* (legs), *Payu* (rectum), *Upastha* (genital organ) ii)Sensory organs or *Jnanendriya*- Eyes (*Cakshu*), Ears (*Karna*), Nose (*Nasika*), Tongue (*Jihwa*), Skin (*Twak*)

iii)Attributes of above sensory organs or *Tanmatra*- Sound (*Shabda*), Touch (*Sparsha*), Form (*Roop*), Taste (*Ras*), Smell (*Gandha*).

iv) Mind, intellect, *Ahamkar* (idea of separate identity)

Total eighteen.

III) **Causal Body** - The 24 Ethos or underlying principles or *Chaturbinshati Tattva*

I) Earth (*Khiti*), Water (*Ap*), Fire (*Tej*)

Air (*Marut*), Space (*Byom*), Speech (*Bak*), Hands (*Pani*), Legs (*Pada*), Anus (*Payu*), Rectum (*Upastha*), Eyes (*Cakshu*), Ears (*Karna*), Nose (*Nasika*), Tongue (*Jihwa*), Skin (*Twak*), Sound (*Shabda*), Touch (*Shabda*), Form (*Roop*), Taste (*Ras*), Smell (*Gandha*), Mind, intellect, *Ahamkar* (idea of separate identity), Unmalifest or Nature or *Abyakta*.

Let us now go through the detailed revelations the Great Yogi Yajnvalkya of ancient India had about what happens to the soul of a commoner and of a self realised yogi at the time of death.

For a common man his coiled up energy at the base of spine termed as *Kundalini Shakti* travel with the help of one of the vital impulse or *Vayu* named *Udan Vayu Through* central channel in spine or *Sushumnapath* along with subtle body or *lingasharir* and causal body or *Kārān déha* to gather at the psychic centre near throat called *Vishuddha Chakra* to attain transcendental subtle body or *Atibāhik deha* and having attained the transcendental body gets released through either eyes, ears, nose or mouth the *Kundalini* goes to the root of the transcendental body becomes inert as it was before and the *Jivatma* (soul in living body) takes the seat at the heart of the transcendental subtle body and the superconscious divinity or *Paramatma* with the purest form of thousand petal lotus reaches the crown of the transcendental subtle body. A common man after death reaches this stage to be born again and again.

But for a liberated soul or *Siddha Yogi,* relinquishment is different. It's not death, it is the ultimate oneness with the supreme being. In the lifetime of *siddha yogi,* the soul is liberated within with radiating effulgence. After leaving the body, the causal body becomes one with the cosmic causal body and the subtle body becomes one with a cosmic subtle body while the gross dissolves into universal gross form. The *Jivatma* (soul in the individual living body) becomes one with the Supreme Consciousness.

The above we get from ***Brihadaranyaka Upanishad***in the following form :

"Yajnavalkyeti Hobach Jatrayang Purusho Mriyat

Udsmat prana: kramantyahot neti neti hobach yajnavalkyohtraiva samavanyanante 3.2.11"—

They become one with the Supreme. This is the meaning of the sentence.

He is freed from the body by assuming various forms. The motion (divine journey) of the liberated soul begins. The self realised *yogis* become conquerors of all the worlds. They never desired for the kingdom of the mundane world, it is said they get the rank of *Brahmā*, the progenitor and enjoy sovereign dominion over the whole world.

They never desired even salvation, but struggled spiritually to be one with the Supreme being.

Now all gods are ready to serve him, looking forward to carrying free souls and to cross the different levels of the magical world.

The soul of a common human being gets the transcendental subtle body after death. The liberated soul does not need a transcendental subtle body. His transcendental gods, viz., the gods carry him away to transcend all levels from this mortal world. Each level has a presiding deity.

Vedanta by the nomenclature indicated the god of those levels.

This is the theory enunciated in *Brahmasutra*.

"Atibahikasthallingat" - Brahma Sutra 4.3.4-

Levels and presiding deities in Vedanta are declared in *Chandogya Upanishad*. The order and names are as follows:

"अथ यदु चैबास्मिश्छब्यं कुर्बन्ति यदिच
नार्चियमेबाभि-संभबस्तयाच्चिर्षोहरह्ण
आपूर्यमानपक्षमापूर्यमानपक्षाद्
यान् षड्दंगेति मासास्तान् मासेभ्यः
संबत्सरंसंबत्सरादादित्यमादित्यच्चन्द्रमसं
चन्द्रमसो बिद्युतं तत्पुरुषोऽमानबः स
एनान् ब्रह्मगमयत्येषदेबपथो ब्रह्मपथ
एतेन प्रतिपाद्यमाना इमंमानबमाबर्तं ना
बर्तन्ते ना बर्तन्ते ॥ छन्दोग्य ४।१५।५

"ath yadu chaibasmishchhabyam kurbanti yadi
cha

narchiyamebabhi-sambhabastayaarchchishohara
hna

aapuryamanpakshamaapuryamanpakshaad

yan shadaudangeti masaastan masebhyah

sambatsaramsambatsaradadityamadityachchand ramasam

chandramaso bidyutam tatpurusho'manabah sa

enan bramagamayatyeshadebapatho bramapath

eten pratipadyamana imanmanabmabarttam na

barttante na barttante || chhandogya 4.15.5

The meaning :

After the death of emancipated *mukta yogi, cremation* and other funeral rites are not at all needed.

They shall be taken to the higher regions by divine forces through the Northern Path or the *uttarayan-marga*, or the *devajana*, the path of light. The *archradi marga* or the *devayana*, the Northern Path of the gods, of the celestials, the path of the liberation of the soul from the bondage of *samsara* or world of desires, is being described. The self realised yogis, they rise to the realm of *Agni* or the deity of (fire) from this world.

They are carried to the higher realm by the deity of flame and from there they are taken up to the still higher realm of the deity of day. There again the matter does not end; they go higher up to the realm of the deity which superintends the bright half of the lunar month. From there again they go higher up to the realms of the deity of the six months during which the sun moves to the north. Then they go higher up to the deity which superintendents over the entire year. Then further they go to the sun, which is a very important halting place, as it is said, in the passage of the soul to liberation. Then the soul goes higher up into the more subtle regions of experience and enjoyment of divine nature, comparable to a cool lunar radiance. Then comes the realm which *Upanishad* calls the flash of lightning (*Vidyut*) represented by its deity. This is not the lightning we see in the sky, but the flash of lightning of the knowledge of Reality. We are on the threshold of the creator, as it were. There the light flashes and then the individuality is about to drop. Effort ceases there and some other takes the soul by hand. A superhuman force begins to work, and Amanab *Purush,* a superhuman being, comes there.

Someone comes and recognises you. The superhuman being catches hold by the hand and leads along the path of light, higher and higher, until they are taken to the realm of creator Himself, the *Brahmalok*. This is the path of light, the path of freedom, the path of liberation.

We find from *Srimad Bhagavad Gita*

- ch 10/sloka 42 :

All the fine and subtlest particles of *PRANA* create Five Great Elements or *Mahabhuta* with the help of *Virjya* or semen. Later it becomes gross to take forms of sensory organs. Thereafter mixing with blood (*Shonit*) it creates the hand, feet etc. and finally creates the ego or idea of separate identity. Thus, life proceeds from subtle stages to gross forms.

Later, when the dissolution occurs, the earth particles enter into the water, the water particles into the fire, the fire particles in air and air particles enter in the void of space or *Akasha*. The *Akasha* particles penetrate into the *Brahman* particle. The world is a part of the *Brahman* particle. This one part of Brahman is rising and sinking down again in *Brahman* itself.

Brahman is infinite; therefore, His centre is everywhere. This centre is like a particle. It is in everything and is called *Anuswarup Brahmakendra* (centre of *brahma* in molecular form). When there is dissolution, all enter into that molecule and in turn it enters into *Brahman*.

When is this condition achieved?-

"If *Panchavatishthante Gnanani with Mansa.*

Buddhishch na bichestet Tamahu:

Paramang Gatim.

Meaning :

When the five senses are fixed with the mind, and the intellect has no effort of its own, that state is called *Parama Gati* by the Wise, this is the state of *Sadhana*.

The world is a part of the molecule of *Brahman*. This part is once rising from *Brahman* and sinking into *Brahman* again. Only a part of *Brahman* is the manifest world, this is illusive truth, the rest is unmanifest. From this unmanifest, *Prana* has arisen and manifested the universe. This unmanifest is the main *Prana*, it has no form. He is the soul of life. He is the immovable *Brahman*.

When it is moved by desire, it is divided into five parts and becomes *Prana, Apana, Samana, Udan, Byan*. The air in the heart is the life by which the living being lives. This is human life. *Brahman*is infinite; therefore, his centre is everywhere.

There is one particle of *Prana* in the sky, two in the air, three in fire, four in water, and five in earth element.

Now the classification of *Prana* :

There are seven divisions of *Prana* - Each again has seven divisions.

Seven *Pranas:- Prabaha (Prana), Sambaha (Apana), Vibaha (Samana), Abaha (Udana), Udbaha (Byan), Paribaha, Parabaha.*

In our body they are known as *Vayu* or Air, in other words they act through nervous impulses. At various psychic centres or *Chakras* in the spine they are considered as petals of lotus. *Prana* in the form of Forty-nine *Vayus* are acting in different numbers at six *chakras*. At *MuladharChakra* or the base there are four *Vayus*, next at *Swadhisthan Chakra* six *Vayus*, then at *Manipur Chakra* there are Ten *Vayus*, then at heart centre *Anahat Chakra* there are Twelve *Vayus*, at throat centre or *Vishuddha Chakra* there are Sixteen *Vayus* and at centre of the eye brows viz. *Ajna Chakra* there is one *Vayu* divided into two to form a total fifty. The upward fifty and downward fifty make hundred and thus acting at ten directions, the final number becomes thousand which is active as Thousand Petalled Lotus (*Sahasrar Padma*) in the pericarp and inner core of the crown. The seven spinal *chakras* or nerve junctions are little known. The relationship between *Prana* and *Chakra* and their names and places of actions with seed *Mantras* are explicitly described below :

आज्ञा चक्र.................................**Ajna Chakra**

बीजाक्षर	वायु
Iniciales	**Name of Vayu**
१। हं क्षं	श्वसिनी टाना महाबल
Ham Ksham	Shwasini Tana Mahabal

विशुद्धचक्र..........**Vishuddha Chakra**

२। अं   परिबह बिहग उड्डियान ऋतबाह

Ang.   Paribaha Bihaga Uddiyan Ṛtabaha

३। आं   परिबह नभःस्वर शब्द शिविति

Aang   Paribaha Navaswar Shabda Shiti

४। इं   परिबह प्राण निमीलन बहिर्गमन त्रिशक्र

Iṁ   Paribaha Pran Nimilan Bahirgaman Trishakra

५। ई।   पराबह मातरिश्वा अणु सत्यजित्

Een   Parabaha Matarishwa Anu Satyajit

६। उं   पराबह अजगतप्राण ब्रहम ऋत

Ung   Parabaha Ajagatpran Brahma Ṛta

७। ऊं   पराबह पबमान ऋतजित्

Oon   Parabaha Pabaman Ṛtajit

८। ऋं   पराबह नभःप्राण प्राणरूपोचित्बाहित्व धाता

Rim   Parabaha Navapran

Pranrupochitbahitwa Dhata

९। ॠं।   पराबह हरि मोक्ष अस्तिमित्र

Rrim.   Parabaha Hari Moksha Astimitra

१०। लं   पराबह सारं मित्र पतिवास

Ling   Parabaha Sarang Mitra Patibas

११। लृं   पराबह स्तनुन सर्बब्यापी मित

Lling   Parabaha Stanun Sarbabyapi Mita

१२। एं   प्रबह श्वसन इन्द्र

En   Prabaha Shwasan Indra

१३। ऐं प्रबह सदागति गमनादो गति

Oing. Prabaha Sadagati Gamanadau Gati

१४। उं प्रबह पृषदश्व स्पर्शशक्ति अदृश्य गति

Um Prabaha Prisadashwa Sparshashakti

Adrishya Gati

१५। ऊं प्रबह गन्धबाह अनुष्ण अशीत ईदृक्ष

Aum Prabaha Gandhabaha Anusna Ashita

Idriksha

१६। अं प्रबह बाह चलान बृतिन

Ang Prabaha Baha Calan Britin

१७। आः प्रबह भोगिकान्त भोगिकाम

Ah Prabaha Bhogikanta Bhogikama

अनाहत चक्र.....Anahatah Chakra or Heart Centre

१८। कं   उद्वह ब्यान जृम्भन आकुञ्चन प्रसारण द्विशक्र

Kang. Udbaha Byan Jrimbhan Akunchan Prasaran

　　　Dwishakra

१९। खं   आबह गन्धबह त्रिशक्र

Khang Aabaha Gandabaha Trishakra

२०। गं   आबह आंशुग शैघ्रं

Gang Abaha Ashuga Shaighrang

२१। घं   आबह मारुत अपात्

Ghang Abaha Maruta Apat

२२। ङं   आबह पवन अपराजित

Uang Abaha Paban Aparajita

२३। चं   आबह फणिप्रिय ऊर्द्धग तिध्रुव

Cang Abaha Phanipriya Urdhagati Druva

२४। छं   आबह निःश्वासक त्वगिन्द्रिय युतिर्घ

Chang Abaha Nihswasak Twagindriya Yutirgha

२५। जं   आबह उदान उद्गीरण सकृत

Jang Abaha Udan Udgiran Sakrit

२६। झं   परिबह अनिल अनुष्ण अजेय

Jhang Paribaha Anila Anusna Ajeya

२७। ञं   परिबह समीरण सुसेन

Yang Paribaha Samiran Susen

२८। टं   परिबह अनुष्ण शीतस्पर्श पसदीक्ष

Tang Paribaha Anusna Shitasparsha

      Pasadiksha

२९। ठं   परिबह सुखाश सुखदा देबदेब

Thang Paribaha Sukhash Sukhada Devadev

मणिपुरचक्र...........................**Manipur Chakra**

३०। डं   बिबह बाति वाक् सभब

Dong Bibaha Bati Vak Savaba

३१। ढं   बिबह अक्षति धारणा अनमित्र

Dhong Bibaha Akshati Dharana Anamitra

३२। णं   बिबह प्रकम्पन कम्पन भीम

Nang Bibaha Prakampan Kampan Bhim

३३। तं   बिबह समान पोषण एकज्यो:ति

Tang. Bibaha Saman Posan Ekajyoti

३४। थं   उद्वह मरुत् सेनजित्

Thang Udbaha Marut Senajit

३५। दं   उद्वह नभःस्वान अपाकज अभियुक्त

Dang Udbaha Navaswan Apakaja Abhiyukta

३६। धं   उद्वह धुनिध्वज आँदिमित

Dhang Udbaha Dhunidhwaj   Andimita

३७। नं   उद्वह कम्पलक्षा सेचनधर्ता

Nang Udbaha Kampalaksha Sechanadharta

३८। पं   उद्वह बास देहब्या पीबिधारण

Pang Udbaha Baas Dehabyapi Bidharan

३९। फं   उद्वह मृगवाहन बिद्युतवरण

Fang Udbaha Mrigabahan Vidyutbaran

स्वाधिष्ठानचक्र....................**Swadhistha Chakra**

४०। बं   संबह चञ्चल उतक्षेपन द्विज्योःति

Bong Sangbaha Chanchal Utkhepan Dwijyoti

४१। भं   संबह पृषतांपति बलंमहाबल

Bhong Sangbaha Prisatanpati Balang

Mahabala

४२। मं   संबह अपान क्षुधाकर अधोगमन एकशक्र

Mong Sabaha Apan Kshudhakar Adhoga Ekashakra

४३। यं   बिबह स्पर्शण स्पर्श विराट

Young Bibaha Sparshan Sparsha Virat

४४। रं   बिबह बात तिर्यकगमन पुराणाय्या

Rang Bibaha Bāta Tirjakgaman Puranajya

४५। लं   बिबह प्रभञ्जन मनपृथक सुमित

Lang Bibaha Prabhanjan Monprithak Sumit

मूलाधारचक्र........................**Muladhar Chakra**

४६। बं   संबह अजगतप्राण जन्ममरण अदृश

Bong   Sangbaha Ajagatprana Janmamaron Adrishya

४७। शं   संबह आवक फेला पुरिमित्र

Shang   Sangbaha Aabak Phela Purimitra

४८। षं   संबह समीर संमित

Sang   Sangbaha Sameer Sangmit

४९। सं   संबह प्रकम्पन मितासन

Ṣang   Sangbaha Prakampan Mitasan

GLOSSARY

(In alphabetical order of Sanskrit words)

Abaha	One of the Life forces
Abyakta	Unmanifest / ineluctable
Ahankar	Idea of separate identity
Amanab	No human
Ananda	Bliss
Anuswarup	Like molecule
Ap	Water
Apana	One of the life forces
Archradi	An existential subtle region through which

	the soul of realised yogi has to pass
Atibāhik	Subtle body after death of ordinary human being
Atma	Self / soul
Avidya	Illusive truth/ Ignorance
Bak	Speech
Brahmakendra	Centre of Brahmans or the supreme being
Brahmalok	Realm of Brahman/ seventh heaven
Brahman	Omniscient, omnipotent, omnipresent supreme consciousness

Buddhi	Intellect
Byan	One of the life forces
Byom	Space
Chaitanya	Cognitive consciousness
Chakra	Centre
Cakshu	Eyes
Chaya path	Path which the Gods select to pass through
Chetana	Consciousness
Chit	Consciousness
Chitta	Conscious vital element
deha	Body

devajana	Divine path
devayana	Divine path
Gandha	Smell
Parama Gati	Final destination / liberation
Iksha	Will
Jihwa	Tongue
Jivatma	Soul in individual
Jnanendriya	Sense organs
Kali / Kalika	A major goddess in Hinduism, associated with time, death, violence, feminine power and motherly love
Kārān	Causal

Karna	Ear
Khshiti / Khiti	Earth
Kripa	Grace
Kundalini	Coiled energy at the base of spine
Kutastha Chaitanya	Eternal consciousness / threshold of consciousness
Linga sharir	Subtle body
Mahabhuta	Great element
Mahakaran	Cause of causal
Manas	Mind or restless Prana
Marga	Road / path
Marut	Air

Maya	Illusive truth
mukta	Liberated
Muladhar	Centre of consciousness at the base of spine
Nasadiya	Not the non-existent
Nasika	Nose
Nirbikalpa	Absolute
Pada	Feet
Padma	Lotus
Pani	Hand
Parabaha	One of the life forces
Para Chaitanya	Supreme consciousness
Parama	Superlative

Paramatma	Supreme Self
Paribaha	One of the life forces
Payu	Anus
Prabaha	One of the life forces
Prana	Life force
Prajna	Inconscience or deep sleep
Purush	Male concept of being
Sadbrahma	Ultimate existential reality
Sadhana	Intense and disciplined esoteric practice for pursuit of self realisation
Shakti	Energy

Samana	One of the life forces
Sambaha	One of the life forces
Sanskar	Impressions of the past
Sat	Existence itself
Sahasrar	Thousand petalled
Shabda	Sound
Shonit	Blood
Siddha yogi	Self-realised sage
Shabda	Sound
Sthula deha	Gross body
Susumna path	Central channel in vertebra

Susupti	Inconscience or deep sleep
Swadhishthan	Centre of consciousness at genital area
Tej	Fire
Turiya	State of super consciousness
Twak	Skin
Udana	One of the life forces
Udbaha	One of the life forces
uttarayan	Ascension
Vaiswanar	Wakefulness
Vayu	Air

Vibaha	One of the life forces
Vidyut	Lightning
Virjya	Semen
Vishuddha	Centre of consciousness in the middle of Throat Centre
Viswatmak	Global
Viswattirna	Extra cosmic
Yogi	Sage